A FUNCTION OF PLAGUES
SURVIVAL POEMS

BETSY WILLIAMSON

Print ISBN: 978-1-66789-225-2
eBook ISBN: 978-1-66789-226-9

Preface

It is one thing to write, and quite another to publish, but in this case I am compelled to do both. I have the sense that I am writing for someone besides myself, although I'm not sure who that is. The last few years have taken a toll on all of us in ways that we may not yet fully appreciate, and have given rise to a profound sense of isolation and unease that is not captured by statistical analyses which attempt to measure our collective progress through anguished times. The truth is in the grit and blood of individual stories; they make the comfort of oversimplification more difficult. These poems describe the recent losses of family, home, and sense of self that I've experienced, and celebrate the moments of understanding that have revealed themselves during the process of adjusting to life after those losses. I'm publishing in the hope that those moments of understanding may be helpful to you. Memory is a powerful and potentially destructive force. Even so, it is crucial to remember, and to remember everything we can, so that we can mark where we have come from. Peace is a process. Safe journeys to everyone.

Betsy Bouldin Williamson

Dedication

To Rose, William,
Charles,
and LeeAnn

May they walk in beauty

Table of Contents

Orphans 1

Home Front, May 1940/2020 2

My Grandmother's Frying Pan 3

Normal 5

Relapse/Free Solo 7

The House 8

The Reporter 10

Independence.. 12

August 13

Nunc Dimittis 14

Mardi Gras.. 15

Secondary Intention.. 17

The Crucifix at St. Agnes 18

Eden 8:20 19

Grief 2 20

The Farmhouse Kitchen Door 21

Things I Never Thought Before You Died................ 22

A Function of Plagues.. 23

On The Creekbed.. 24

Signs 25

Orphans

What happens when the altar of the heart
Can hold no further stories?
Do they fall like seeds onto the earth?
Do they ride the wind, investing surfaces
With meaning—the book caressed,
The venerated shirt?
They cannot propagate without a host
Neither can we safely lock them away.

At what point do we feel
The cage filled to bursting, and simply say:
I turn you out. I have no milk for you.
Seek other homes.
When the heart is full and no rain comes,
What happens to the soul?
Even locusts search for green
But only in their time
And not when havoc falls like hailstones.

I gather in between the sun and moon,
Winnowing what I can
Waiting for signs of gentle soil,
To bury what I must
And tend its increase.

Home Front, May 1940/2020

I forget, before rising in the morning,
that I am not the one entrenched
and that the peril is now borne
by my students, sent too soon this brazen spring,
to a harrowing of their own.
It is easier by far to grip a gun
than bow my head and grasp the truth.
I am not suited to this fight.
Gnarled hands and mirror make it plain.
I am a relic who prays,
a seer of past and future days.
My proving ground at this age
is the wresting of fish and potatoes
to fill the bellies of those
who fly and sail over the deep
and creep into pitiless hedgerows.
I listen to the wireless every night
and smell the dirt and taste the salt
before I rise, turn out the light,
and climb the tired stairs,
sending those stranded on foreign shores
an armada in my dreams.

My Grandmother's Frying Pan

I remember making eggs for you
in another time before we fled,
with my grandmother's frying pan—
one hundred years of seasoned cast iron.
I served them on my mother's earthenware
in the time before
the wind shrieked through
and water, oddly, dirtied everything.

Now, setting down the melamine,
I think of our familiar things
swept to sea or into other lives
so many strange comminglings
such perverse creativity.
Displaced, we are debris
as surely as our belongings

I want my boundaries back.
All colors mixed revert to shades of black—
black, like that frying pan
which rendered fat and smothered greens
for my family's strongest women

I remember that a bit of iron
finds its way into the meal
just as they who fed me still transmit
a smile, a turn of phrase, some scratch of DNA
through all this time, to the one
now mourning a frying pan.
Not all that iron or grit is gone.

Normal

It was a normal tourist visit
with the normal amount of weapons and violence
following a perfectly normal rally
on an ordinary normal day.
The besieged barricaded their chambers
in the normal way.

It was normal
for my mother to die without her family
because citizens exercised their freedoms,
shared their arrogant air,
and separated us from her.
It is normal for liberty to trample memory.

It was normal to recognize
that the only bodies close to each other
were corpses consigned to freezers
or burning together on pyres.
It is normal to disbelieve your eyes.

It was normal to view
my broken father through a window
and choose the news
whose narrative I could bear.
It is normal to ignore
what you do not wish to hear.

Normal.

We insisted it be normal.

And so it became.

Relapse/Free Solo

You have learned, since you have summitted before,
that the sheer face is falsehood.
That mountains, like mourning, are not monoliths
that there is grace in spaces
which offer footholds and intimate time.

Expansive seconds of respite and searching,
the next traverse, the hand outstretched,
the blessed ledge, the breath drawn and given.
No room remains for terror or illusion.
This climb, though not your choice, is now your passion.

You have been shaped for this embrace.
Time erodes both rock and bone
and fits you for each other

so that even if you choose to fly
the stone will still remember.

The House

No one had ever lived there before.
I remember the fresh paint smell
when the house, and I, were new
and the rooms echoed back my voice
from their emptiness.
I was frightened by the hollowness.

No one lives there now
except the box of ancestors
gently mouldering upstairs
under the years of debris
that layered in like ash,
the small interments of the days.
A closet offers up both hobby horse and cane.
The photo-faded newlyweds lie smiling,
tucked among the gap-toothed consequences
of one fine, early morning in June.
What is near is what was far away.

There are no echoes anymore.
There is hardly room for air,
however memory-thick and aged,
to sustain the work of dismantling
what has been long unhinged.

And I consider how I am become
the destroyer of this home,
and wonder what essential thing removed
will cause this house to sigh and fold.
I wish that I'd been told, if anyone could,
which weight-bearing beam
would make the brightest flame.

The Reporter

This merciless June, I am in hibernation,
denned up, nursing wounds,
Mourning one cub dead, another wasting,
shrouding them with stories,
curled around the loss.
I've ignored your noise,
left your calls unanswered,
I am deaf to your cause
and stuporous with grief.
Still you push in,
armed with feigned concern
and the public's right to know....what, exactly?
I am not deceived by this show
of righteous belief.
You want my family's story for a trophy.
It will cover your floor, hang on your wall,
gather dust anonymously
while you prowl for your next prey.

I have left my body.
Somehow, from a high corner of the porch,
I see myself, now eight feet tall, bared teeth and claws,
Snarling, hurling you into the yard
With the force of a voice I've been
Waiting my whole life to use.
You retreat, amazed, confused

As I pursue you to the street.

I could have justified your blood
And chewed your marrow cold, that day.

How quickly we transform
from predator to food,
in this random kingdom of the inhumane.

Here on this earth, all stations turn.

Someone will harvest you, in time.

Independence

When embers kindle into flame,
they do not discuss their sovereignty.
The storm winds blend,
nameless into name,
then elemental once again.
The life you claim never was your own.
You are the seed of others' dreams,
the shared currency of days.
A river, charged with melted snow,
will not obey its ordinary banks.
The fullness is too much.
Neither can you contain your course.
Life swells. Memories tumble by.
Gravity and memory are one force,
too much to bear alone, but comforting
to be carried on—
always the pull, the brief abandon,
change of form, return to mossy earth.
If any part of this is death
it also falls away.

August

The invitation is to stay—
Weightless and waiting under the
deafening upstart sun
who is so mighty in these days
that, even unseen, he warms.
The heat erases the horizon
and there is only time senselessly ticking
for when sand is everywhere
what use is an hourglass?
The unanswered hand
holds no benediction.

But in the unblinking stare of afternoon
the seduction is undone.
There is the briefest flickering,
a lengthening of evening,
a faltering of sun.
The old clock in the deepening dark
chimes slow
but runs fast.
The leaves, the brittle bones,
begin their rattling dance.

Nunc Dimittis

Blessed is the dust outgrown
the ritual you shall not have
Blessed is the plan undone.

Blessed is the past laid down
I will be your open grave
Blessed is the dust outgrown.

Blessed is the greening wood
the watchful tree you learned to love
Blessed is the plan undone.

Blessed is the word unsaid
a peace withheld from you to give
Blessed is the dust outgrown.

Blessed are the numbered dead
whose common history you lived
blessed is the plan undone.

Blessed is the hymn unsung
and the memory of song
Blessed is the dust outgrown
Blessed is the plan undone.

Mardi Gras

this day we devour
purple desserts. lost color
crowds past the curb—
purple, I have missed the most.
there is no wind today, but if there were
we'd wait anyway,
because we're still here
and this is our parade.

somewhere in the ring there is a golden son
wishing to be uncovered.
we do this every year.
your pirate eye gleams
towards my skeleton. my bones covet
more glitter.
I carry a torch, not a ladder
and you hoist on your non-parrot shoulder
the green-eyed girl you've fallen for.
every year we go
because this is our parade.

next year let's ride this route
our much-beloved parade,
in deep violet disguise,
throwing wildly to child and friend
all we've hoarded through these years.
we'll spy the green-eyed girl
and toss a strand of something bright
and useless
that her older hand may later caress
and wonder at how much it meant.

Secondary Intention

When the wound is wide, the edge is everything.
All healing comes from that horizon
while the damaged deep still reels.
Vessels smuggling fuel and sacrifice snake in,
scaffolds stake their stubborn beachheads,
an age of chaos fades, its ruins overgrown.
We will become Mayan, Roman,
a scar that needs interpretation.

Catastrophe turns into story—
and stories, though they echo,
have an end.

yet, in these present predawn days
we wake in dark avulsion,
searching for the scrim of light to come.
Waiting to be invaded
and healed again.

The Crucifix at St. Agnes

Oh contorted Christ,
anguished kite hovering over the altar,
you do not need to rise for me.

It is enough that you began
as perfectly as my ancestors
that you slept innocently
amongst mass murders
that you grew confidently, wept bitterly,
laughed, walked your path.
That your pain was shared
and ended.
That you felt in your body
the passage of power into the void
as I can now imagine it.

I will curl up beside you
as an animal in the ancient night,
seeking only warmth and form
with no thought or need of more.

Eden 8:20

among the green vines, strung with morning diamonds,
I find a prize:
tiny red suns, hot in the hand,
each a factory of memory,
the memory of light from my natal star.
It is too much to comprehend,
how sunspot transmutes to seed,
this dissonance of size.
All things are reduced—
space, time, separation, fear—
as if I can hear this garden breathe
while swelling pods nod in the nascent shade.

What I knew of you
I can no longer hold.
You're as obscure as God
unbound by any form in root or bud—
forsaking every shrine I build
as if it were too small a shoe.

What did I love?
The timeless child, assured adult,
unsteady elderly?
Not one scene, but many.
I loved the narrative.
This humming I still hear.
Not the dear wreckage left behind.

Grief 2

No one can say we were not warned.
But how many times has catastrophe stalked us
And pounced instead on a neighbor's less wary friend,
leaving us to ponder our good providence?

There was a rustling darkness.
We went interior as if it mattered.
A green sky and then a rising,
Not dread so much as exaltation.
The whole house lifted and every atom in it
Chorused the passing energy.

Dropped to earth off our foundation,
Not one thing unshifted.
No one knows
how we survived.

The Farmhouse Kitchen Door

Here is a door no longer fitted to its frame.
weathered to a weary shape, by heat
and flood and wind, by the happy
slamming of little hands
abandoning their safe limits,
leaving a tether for return.

Oh, we were countries then,
bronzed in dirt and sun,
boundaries of days and territories drawn
until we were called in.
The door defined our dynasties.

Now aged and unrepentant, more a portal,
lacking all discrimination.
Nothing will ever close again
though the latch still sounds
its minor second.
And this is good.
There is no keep left to defend.
The gift of light and air is not surrender.

Things I Never Thought Before You Died

How could time be truant to its linear task
of keeping everything from happening at once?
The days have no bars, their contents escape.
In a monotony of gravity, nothing stays in place.

How could the great wide world implode
carrying you into its damned yawning black hole
while, while, while
well, you know the rest.
You said you learned a lot before you left.

How did the line of actual control morph from map into
a dare drawn deep within a soul?
You shrewdly threw that bone to me to gnaw on.
I'm bloodied to the gums.
You, after some reflection, rose above a sun-drenched room.

How does joy grow like petals on a creeping vine?
And grateful yet, what's left for me to wrap my arms around?
I bless with all the voice I have, but carry no one's dreams.
How and when do time and all its rituals resume?
I'm just another outlaw until then.

A Function of Plagues

Come back
come back to me in sleep
where dust can dare dream of itself.
Unfurl the crumpled canvas of your life—
a galaxy, whose arc is only traceable at night.

I will praise the fluency of blues, the bright
Cartesian stars pulsing through, each murmuring:
here we are. This is who we were, among the multitude.
Here is the sinuous mural of our days,
Here our passionate travels graphed.
It is a function of plagues, a calculus of loss,
this fearsome map of passages.
The tender, implacable curve will hold.

I lie marveling
in a fallow field,
honoring your constellation,
moving only with the seasons of the earth,
wondering, wondering
if I will ever have wondered
enough.

On The Creekbed

through some season's sleight of hand,
the south bluff glows all day.
the creek, slipping past its shaded bend,
sighs unseen into irresistible light.

Muddled gravel, red clay,
both mutter under boot.
A hollowed bone
becomes the wind's flute.
The fallen trees, and rocks worn patient,
do not care what they once were.
History and destiny are the same to them,
arms already arched downstream,
moss bearding a long-settled boulder
calmly crumbling to another form.

Frenzied leaves, late for an appointment,
curl around each ripple in this dwindled current.
Soon
they'll find the sun
and wait there for the trees, the nimble stones,
the bones now singing in the stirring air.

Signs

for me, wildflowers and jay-songs;
for you, perhaps, the knowing smile
of the half-grown child
or fruit bending its fragrant offering
from your favorite tree.
the noticing gives notice:
a part of us has joined the dance.
Not the steps we learned in youth
but a whirling large enough to hold all loss.

See how the morning light becomes
your prayer shawl, worn close
in its beseeching embrace?
the canopy has come down.
a tender melody from your own heart
answers what is gently, gently asked.

Yes, you will break.
You will break like dawn
and in supple grace
rejoice, and wander blessed
as one loved in the world,
loved of the world.